Who Helps Dad?

CONTENTS

NATIONAL GEOGRAPHIC   Hampton-Brown

School Publishing

g

Sounds for g, d, v, r

Look at the picture. Read the words.

van

rag

Dad

gas

2

High Frequency
Words

| get |
| help |
| of |
| put |
| we |
| work |

Key Words

Look at the picture. Read the sentences.

Dad and I at Work

1. I **help** Dad.
2. **We** **work** on the van.
3. Dad can **get** a can **of** gas.
4. I **put** a mat in the van.

> What help did Dad get?

Phonics Games

NGReach.com

3

My Dad

by Lada Kratky
illustrated by Jomike Tejido

I like to help my dad.

We get a plant.

We put it in the van.

We get rid of weeds.

We dig a hole.

We put the plant in the hole.

I like to help my dad. ❖

Sounds for g, d, v, r

Read these words.

van	rag	rat	tag	dad
mad	sad	pig	dig	tan

Find the words that start with **r**.
Then find words with **g**, **d**, and **v**.
Use letters to build them.

Talk Together

Choose words from the box to talk about what you see in the picture.

The _pig_ is _sad_.

11

Words with Short o

o

Look at the pictures. Read the words.

Example:

d**o**g

m**o**m

h**o**t d**o**g

m**o**p

h**o**g

f**o**g

12

High Frequency
Words

get
help
of
put
we
work

Key Words

Look at the picture. Read the sentences.

My Dog

1. **We** have a lot **of** **work**.
2. Can my dog **help**?
3. My dog can **get** the cap.
4. Dad can **put** on the cap.

What can Dad do with the cap?

Phonics Games

NGReach.com

13

Mop, the Dog

by Lada Kratky
illustrated by Mike Reed

My dad has a dog.

His dog is Mop.

Dad has a lot of work.

Dad gets Mop to help.

Mop can help Dad with the hogs.

fog

Mop can help Dad in the fog.

cot

Can Mop help Dad nap?

Not if Mop hops on the cot! ❖

Words with Short o

Read these words.

sit	sip	mom	dog	cat
hop	dad	fan	hog	nap

Find the words with short **o**.
Use letters to build them.

h　o　p

Talk Together

Choose words from the box above
to tell your partner a story about
the picture.

The **mom**
can **fan** .

A Lot of Work

Look at the pictures with a partner. Take turns reading the clues. Then find each person.

1. Mom has a mop.
2. Dad hops on the van.
3. Tom gets rags.
4. Pam pats the dog.
5. Don puts on a cap
6. Viv sits and sips.